*Praise for*
Bagua Linked Palms

"Kent Howard not only has the experience in Bagua to write this, he also has the intelligence and discrimination to do the translation justice. I know of no better person in the English- or Chinese-speaking world for the task. I hope and expect this text to be the definitive one on Wang Shujin for many years to come."

—ALLEN PITTMAN, author of *Walking the I Ching:*
*The Linear Ba Gua of Gao Yi Sheng*

"Here at last is the late Master Wang Shujin's introduction to the sublime art of Bagua Zhang in English! We all owe a debt to Kent Howard for this valuable contribution to the martial arts archive."

—MARNIX WELLS, author of *Scholar Boxer:*
*Cháng Nâizhou's Theory of Internal Martial Arts and the Evolution of Taijiquan*

"Wang Shujin's *Bagua Linked Palms* ranks as one of the most influential Bagua training manuals ever written. This work is an outstanding addition to the historical scholarship concerning Wang Shujin and with its numerous clear photos, it is equally valuable for those seeking practical instruction in Wang's Bagua."

—BRIAN L. KENNEDY, author of *Chinese Martial Arts Training Manuals:*
*A Historical Survey*

# Bagua
## Linked Palms

## Wang Shujin

*Translated by* Kent Howard and Chen Hsiao-Yen
*Commentary by* Kent Howard

BLUE SNAKE BOOKS
BERKELEY, CALIFORNIA

Published by Blue Snake Books

Blue Snake Books' publications are distributed by
North Atlantic Books
P.O. Box 12327
Berkeley, California 94712

Cover and book design by Susan Quasha
Photography by Scott Hamm
Photo restoration by Gary Baugh
Printed in the United States of America

*Bagua Linked Palms* is sponsored by the Society for the Study of Native Arts and Sciences, a nonprofit educational corporation whose goals are to develop an educational and cross-cultural perspective linking various scientific, social, and artistic fields; to nurture a holistic view of arts, sciences, humanities, and healing; and to publish and distribute literature on the relationship of mind, body, and nature.

North Atlantic Books' publications are available through most bookstores. For further information, visit our websites at www.northatlanticbooks.com and www.bluesnakebooks.com or call 800-733-3000.

PLEASE NOTE: The creators and publishers of this book disclaim any liabilities for loss in connection with following any of the practices, exercises, and advice contained herein. To reduce the chance of injury or any other harm, the reader should consult a professional before undertaking this or any other martial arts, movement, meditative arts, health, or exercise program. The instructions and advice printed in this book are not in any way intended as a substitute for medical, mental, or emotional counseling with a licensed physician or healthcare provider.

Library of Congress Cataloging-in-Publication Data

Wang, Shujin, 1904-1981.
 [Ba gua lian huan zhang. English]
 Bagua linked palms / Wang Shujin ; translated by Kent Howard and Chen Hsiao-Yen ; commentary by Kent Howard.
   p. cm.
 ISBN 978-1-58394-264-2
 1. Hand-to-hand fighting, Oriental. I. Howard, Kent, 1950- II. Title.

GV1112.W384513 2009
796.815'5—dc22

2008055692

3 4 5 6 7 8 9 SHERIDAN 15 14 13 12 11

To Huang Jinsheng
*For sharing your gift*

# Acknowledgments

A project such as this would not be possible without the help and cooperation of a great many people. I would like to express my gratitude to Scott Hamm for being a great workout partner and a fine photographer. Also, thanks to graphic designer and fellow Bagua enthusiast Gary Baugh for doing a terrific job cleaning up the photos in Wang Shujin's original text and for converting all of our photos for publication. My appreciation goes out to project editor Erin Wiegand, copy editor Christopher Church, and designer Susan Quasha at North Atlantic Books for their tireless efforts in guiding this project from formulation to fruition. I would also like to express my thanks to Jess O'Brien in Berkeley, California, for promoting the book proposal.

On the research side, a big thank you goes out across the water to John Kavanagh in Ireland for his interest and support and for introducing me to his teacher in England, Marnix Wells. Marnix, a former student of Wang Shujin, was very generous in sharing his recollections and expertise. I am also greatly indebted to my other long-distance friends and collaborators who contributed so much to this project: Allen Pittman in France; Brian and Elizabeth Kennedy in Taiwan; Patrick Hodges, my teacher and friend in Hawaii; and Manfred Rottman in California, another direct student of Wang Shujin.

Thanks go to my friend Craig Butler in Hong Kong, also a former pupil of Wang Shujin, for lending me his first-edition copy of Wang's book and for helping me to negotiate Chinese fonts and Pinyin etiquette. I also owe a debt of gratitude to my good friend Robert Greenebaum in Massachusetts, for talking me into doing this project in the first place, and to the excellent Brian Williams, for helping to get us off to a good start.

Finally, I would like to recognize my teacher in Taiwan, Huang Jinsheng, a former disciple of Wang Shujin and himself a master teacher of the Dao, for his generosity of spirit and great patience in teaching a muddleheaded *lao wai* the intricacies of his art. If I have neglected to mention any other contributors to this modest effort, I assure you it is not out of ingratitude but rather the demands of brevity.

KENT HOWARD
Chico, California
March 2009

# Contents

# Translator's Introduction

We are pleased to bring to a general readership this seminal work by one of the great martial artists of the twentieth century, Wang Shujin. Master Wang was one of the foremost exponents of Chinese internal martial arts in Taiwan and Japan during the 1960s and 1970s, when China was still essentially closed to the rest of the world. In fact, Wang was the first Chinese instructor to introduce Taiji Quan, Xingyi Quan, and Bagua Zhang to a receptive though hitherto tradition-bound Japanese public. In all, Wang taught over two thousand students in Japan and Taiwan and established schools in both countries that are still thriving today. Around this same time, Wang Shujin was also introduced to Western readers through the literary efforts of American martial artists Donn Draeger and Robert W. Smith.

This is the first complete translation of Wang's introductory book on Bagua Zhang, *Bagua Linked Palms*, which he printed privately in Taiwan in 1978. Wang also wrote a second book that presented a more advanced form in his Bagua curriculum titled *Bagua Swimming Body Palms*. It was published by the Taiwanese Ministry of Education around the time of his death in 1981.

This book is an attempt to offer a faithful rendering of Wang Shujin's beginning Bagua Zhang form. The form is one of the simplest and most orthodox methods to be found within the Bagua Zhang pantheon; as such, it cries out for wider dissemination in a martial arts world much polluted by modern heresies such as Wushu. Therefore we sought to reproduce the original Chinese text by presenting it in the same chapter order from start to finish with the original photographs and illustrations. We have not omitted any material or edited the text beyond necessity as demanded by coherence.

For the sake of clarity, and to expand those topics that were given only a cursory treatment by the author, clearly marked commentary sections are introduced at appropriate points in the text. Great care was taken to make sure the supporting material was as bereft of personal opinion or revisionism as possible. Another feature included was the addition of over one hundred sequential photographs of the form in an effort to supplement the meager number of illustrations found in the original text.

Wang Shujin was a man of few words of both tongue and pen. He wrote plainly and directly on his subject. Still, his medium of communication, the Chinese language, has proven to be a linguistic minefield for many an undisciplined translator. Some elemental vocabulary found within the text, such as *Dao* or *Qi*, could have easily invoked prosaic flights taking on lives of their own. Where explanations of terminology became so expansive as to interrupt the flow of the narrative, the offending definitions were banished to a glossary at the end of the book along with Chinese equivalents of personal names and place names. Where clarity was essential and brevity amenable, English definitions of Chinese terms were placed in parentheses within the text. When appropriate for readability, the order was reversed.

Wang Shujin was a dynamic and charismatic individual, and he garnered a devoted following of students, disciples, and admirers during his long life. Indeed, there are many around the world that still revere him and continue to promulgate his philosophical and martial teachings to this day. To those insiders, there may not be many revelations to be found in this book. Our purpose in translating and expanding this work was to introduce Wang Shujin's Bagua Zhang to a wider public, and perhaps a new generation, who may be unfamiliar with his great art. It was with great respect for the material and the man that we embarked on this effort. We apologize in advance for the inevitable gaffes and omissions, and we welcome any comments or suggestions readers may have.

# Author's Preface

Bagua Zhang, Xingyi Quan, and Taiji Quan have always been considered internal martial arts in China. When Bagua Zhang began and who created it are the subject of debate. But it is inarguable that previous sages have passed it on, crystallized from their hearts and blood, for generations. It was not until the waning years of the Manchu Dynasty and the efforts of Master Dong Haiquan that Bagua Zhang became well known to common people.

In the beginning Master Dong taught only in the Imperial Palace; it was only in later years that he began accepting students from outside. From that time, however, his door was crowded with disciples "like a noisy market." Among his more famous students were Cheng Tinghua, Yin Fu, Liang Zhenpu, Sung Yongxiang, Shi Baoshan, Liu Fengchun, Li Cunyi, and my teacher, Zhang Zhaodong. Each in turn had their own disciples who in succession helped Bagua Zhang to flourish.

In the spring of 1923, at the age of eighteen, I began studying Bagua Zhang and Xingyi Quan in the school of Master Zhang. In 1934 I also studied Zhan Zhuang [Post Standing] with Master Zhang's martial arts brother Wang Xiangzhai. They were two of the best-known teachers of their era—highly skilled, morally irreproachable, and strict disciplinarians. In 1939 I also studied Bagua Zhang for over a year with Xiao Haibo. Master Xiao had previously studied at Mt. Luo Jia, about fifty miles from Mt. Ermei. When I learned from him he was already over ninety years of age. As a teacher he was gentle, scholarly, and patient—truly a model for our generation! I originally studied a form of Silian Quan [Four Continuous Fists]. The hand movements were very similar to Chen-style Taiji Quan.

In 1951, three years after arriving in Taiwan, I happened to meet my former martial arts senior, Chen Panling. We shared a great deal of martial knowledge with each other. We examined techniques already mastered, for their good and bad points, and transformed our combined experience into a new style of Chen Taiji Quan. Master Chen has since passed on and is greatly missed.

There is a saying: Establish virtue and honor as your guiding principle, and your will and purpose will be bound as metal to stone. Thus I took the name of Shujin ["establish virtue like metal"] which has often been an inspiration to strengthen my resolve. I have practiced my art for these many years, avoiding social entanglements, following a strict vegetarian regimen, meditating daily, practicing Buddhism, and, after my daily labors, practicing martial arts as my sole entertainment.

In the summer of 1948, in an effort to escape social upheaval, I traveled through Shanghai and on to Taiwan, where I established the Cheng Ming Martial Arts School. There, in the city of Taichung, I taught Bagua Zhang, Xingyi Quan, and Taiji Quan. Over the years, I have instructed hundreds of students from all over Taiwan. Many of them have remained faithful to their art and their teacher for these many years.

In 1959 I traveled to Japan, where an old acquaintance of mine, Wu Botang, gave me an introduction to Toyama Izumi, head of the Jodo Association of Japan, who invited me to teach Taiji Quan in his dojo. I later taught Xingyi Quan and Bagua Zhang also, for eight years. In 1963 I traveled to Japan again upon accepting an invitation from the Japanese Goju-ryu Karate Association's Central Karate Dojo. I brought along a disciple and taught there for over two years. In 1966 I made another trip to Japan to teach at Korin Temple in Minato-ku, Tokyo, for over one year.

By 1976 I had made eight visits to Japan. In total, I have taught over twelve hundred students in Japan. Among these were overseas Chinese, Japanese, and foreign tourists. Many of those students were themselves masters and brought with them high-level skills in Judo, Karate, and Aikido. Altogether, both in Taiwan and Japan, the number of my students reached eighteen hundred.

I have had no other desire but to work hard to disseminate and perpetuate my teachers' school of boxing. I am now seventy-four years old. What more can I ask but that this stream of my art flows on forever to benefit our people. Be not selfish but ever virtuous and at ease with people. Nourish your own spirit but consider well the views of others. Hold to the middle path and find joy and contentment in your later years.

At the behest of my students, I have written this *Bagua Linked Palms* reference manual for training. My fervent hope, in setting these teachings down in writing, is to avoid contending interpretations and allow all to follow the correct method. When I was young I learned from famous teachers, and for decades I have been following this great moral and physical Way. Chinese martial arts are varied and profound, and their teachings are highly sophisticated. I was a slow and clumsy learner and caught but one tenth of my master's teachings. How dare I show my ineptitude to all and be ridiculed! And yet, my students have been so enthusiastic that it is difficult to disappoint them.

Chinese martial arts are an integral part of our cultural heritage. As a member of the Taiwan National Committee on Martial Arts, I feel I have the duty to promote them. I submit this book in order to organize my teachings and present them to the world. I cast forth this brick that others may respond with jade, and together our martial brothers throughout the world will unite in the propagation of our great national art for the benefit of all.

This text is written in a plain style with separate discussions; all movements are analyzed and explained to provide utmost clarity and clear instruction. Individual sections may be practiced separately until you are familiar [with them], and then they may be practiced as a whole. When the upper and lower are balanced and adjusted, the inner and outer united, the right and left harmonized, then it is possible to understand the mysteries. This book was rushed into publication and may contain errors and omissions within. If any are found, please correct me.

WANG SHUJIN OF TIANJIN
Taichung, Taiwan, August 1978

*Zhang Zhaodong*

*Wang Shujin*

Wang Shujin was considered by many people who knew him as, borrowing Winston Churchill's famous phrase, "a riddle wrapped in a mystery inside an enigma." The riddle, if a touch of mirth may be allowed to creep in, may have been: What is five-foot-eight, two hundred fifty pounds, and moves like a cat? The mystery was where and from whom he learned his martial arts, and why he taught what he did. The enigma was, quite simply, his jealously guarded personal life.

Little is known of Wang Shujin's early life in Mainland China before his exodus to the province of Taiwan. He was forty-four years old when he arrived on the island in 1948, and he had, no doubt, lived a full and eventful life up to then. It was said he left a wife and children behind when he fled ahead of the Communist advance on the coastal cities of Tianjin and Shanghai. There are also several conflicting stories, told by people who claimed to have known him well, concerning the details of his early career: one person said he had been a trader in an import-export company; another remarked that he was formerly a carpenter; and yet another slandered him, on the occasion of his memorial service no less, with the accusation that he had been a mere noodle vendor. But why would someone involved in any of the aforementioned professions feel the need to flee from persecution by the Communist authorities?

The answer is that Wang Shujin was no ordinary businessman, or at least not entirely so. Whatever his early career path may have been, he was first and foremost a high-level leader in a secret society called Yi Guan Dao (Way of One Unity). Yi Guan Dao was not a triad, as some have thought, but rather a syncretic religious sect that adhered to Daoist and Buddhist principles and beliefs. It originally began in Shandong Province under the name of Xian Tian Da Dao (Great Way of Pre-Heaven).

Yi Guan Dao was unique in that it attracted a great many powerful people in China, including politicians, prominent businessmen, and martial artists. It is of special interest that many famous Bagua Zhang practitioners, such as Sun Xikun, Wu Mengxia, Zhang Zhaodong, and Zhang Junfong were reputed to have been members of the sect. Since Dong Haiquan himself was a Daoist, and given the strong Daoist associations found in Bagua Zhang practice, it is logical that many of its adherents would be attracted to such an organization.

Indeed, it was the Yi Guan Dao organization that helped to facilitate Wang Shujin's transition to exile in Taiwan. Zhou Yisen, a local leader of the movement on the island, traveled to Shanghai from Taipei in 1947 to attend the funeral of a famous Yi Guan Daoist luminary. There Zhou met Wang Shujin, who was representing the Tianjin chapter at the service, and took a liking to him. Zhou wanted to bring someone of Wang's stature to Taiwan to help promote Yi Guan Dao activities on the island. Wang apparently took Zhou up on his offer the following year when his options for remaining on the Mainland became severely limited. Wang arrived in the Taiwanese port city of Keelung in 1948 about one year before the government and army of the Republic of China fled to the island one step ahead of the pursuing Communist forces.

The Nationalist authorities considered Yi Guan Dao to be, quoting an official government reference book, "an outlawed quasi-religious secret society." Today it is more widely accepted as a secretive but more or less mainstream religious group of less sinister purpose than earlier conceived. However, in Wang's time there appeared to be many reasons for Yi Guan Daoists to keep their activities cloistered and their ceremonies sealed. Many friends, acquaintances, and students of Wang Shujin, right up to the end of his life, knew little about his involvement in the sect.

To return to Wang Shujin's early experience in learning martial arts, it has been established that he studied in Zhang Zhaodong's school, but not necessarily that he learned directly under Zhang. Wang studied in the school for eight years; however, Zhang died in his seventh year of attendance. It is known that another teacher Wang mentioned in his Author's Preface, Xiao Haibo, was invited to teach at the school after Zhang's passing. Wang Shujin appeared to have been very impressed with Xiao. Wang mistakenly wrote that Xiao was over ninety years old when he studied under him. Xiao Haibo died in 1954 at the age of ninety-one; he was around sixty-eight when he taught Wang.

As to what Wang Shujin learned under Zhang and Xiao, one may only speculate. Zhang Zhaodong was a student of Dong Haiquan, and was certainly quite adept at Bagua Zhang, but he was probably most famous for his expertise in Xingyi Quan. Xiao Haibo, on the other hand, was reputed to have studied a derivation of Bagua Zhang. However, Wang Shujin's only clue concerning Xiao's curriculum was a cryptic comment about having learned Silian Quan (Four Continuous Fists), and that it was somewhat like Chen Taiji Quan.

After arriving in Taiwan, Wang Shujin initially lived and worked out with his martial arts "brother," Zhang Junfong. Zhang had been Wang's senior in the training halls of Tianjin but his subordinate in Yi Guan Dao circles. It is difficult to know what the two shared with each other, but Zhang later became a well-known instructor in his own right and taught the famous Hong brothers, Yimian and Yixiang.

Shortly after an initial period of settling in to life on the island, Wang moved to Taichung City to take up his duties as the Central Taiwan coordinator of the Yi Guan Dao community. It was there that he was introduced to Chen Panling. Chen had come to Taiwan with the Nationalist forces and had close ties to the new government. On the Mainland, Chen had been fairly well known as one of the prime movers involved in setting up a national curriculum for the martial arts, and he had helped to develop a combined, synthetic style of Taiji which later took his name. Wang Shujin formed a liaison with the influential Chen and later became the chief instructor in his loosely formed "school."

Soon after arriving in Taichung, Wang Shujin went into business and, over the years, became quite prosperous. At some point in the mid-1950s he began to conduct classes in a Taichung park; he also taught a larger class that was sponsored by the recreation commission in neighboring Zhanghua City. Wang's curriculum at that time consisted of Zhan Zhuang standing meditation, a version of Chen Panling's Taiji Quan, Wang's Xingyi Quan, and Bagua Zhang. His beginning Bagua form was the same one that Chen Panling offered in his school. It is not known who taught it to whom. Wang Shujin also taught other higher-level Bagua routines, such as Bagua Swimming Body Palms, that were derived wholly from his previous study and practice on the Mainland.

Wang Shujin first came to the attention of the world outside of Tianjin and Taiwan when he was invited to teach in Japan. There he met a couple of men who would be instrumental in introducing Wang Shujin and his art to the English reading public: Donn Draeger, himself the most accomplished Westerner ever to learn martial arts directly from the Japanese, and Robert W. Smith, a CIA agent and pugilist who later became well known, along with Donn, as an interpreter of Asian fighting arts; in fact they cowrote a vast compendium of the same title.

Wang's exploits in Japan became the stuff of legend. There is insufficient space herein to recount all of the stories that were told, and are still told, of his encounters with Japanese and Western fighters. The outcome was always the same, however. Many of the vanquished bowed down and became his students; those for whom defeat was not a viable career option merely stayed away. There is one fact among tale and saga that has yet to be refuted by anyone over these many years: he was never known to be humbled or defeated in any trial or contest. That is an enviable record indeed.

It is fascinating to note that martial arts were not the most important aspect of Wang Shujin's long and eventful public life in Taiwan and Japan. His devotion to Yi Guan Dao took precedence over all other activities. In fact, Wang remains more famous as the person who introduced Yi Guan Dao to the Japanese than for his martial exploits. Thanks in no small part to his efforts, and those who followed him, such as his disciple Huang Jinsheng, there are now thousands (some say hundreds of thousands) of Yi Guan Dao members throughout the Japanese islands. To his devoted followers, that was indeed his shining legacy.

After many years of traveling back and forth between Taiwan and Japan, Wang Shujin finally began to tire of the grind and, as his health began to fail, retired to his Taichung residence. He continued to teach in the local park and in his Cheng Ming martial arts school, however, until the effects of diabetes and other debilitating ailments severely limited his activities. Wang Shujin died in 1981 and was buried in a great lotus-shaped coffin on a hilltop overlooking the school founded in his name in Caotun, Taiwan. To this day his students and grand-students, joined by admirers from around the world, still perform annual memorial rites in his honor at his graveside.

*Figure 1: 1976 reunion of Wang Shujin's students on Bagua Hill in Zhanghua, Taiwan. Seated center, Wang Shujin; seated left, Huang Jinsheng; standing back row left, Wang Fulai, head instructor of Cheng Ming*

# A Brief Introduction to Master Dong Haiquan

It is said that Master Dong was a born in Wenan County in present day Hebei Province. As a young man, he loved to gamble and often got himself into trouble. Finally he had to flee his home to live in the capital, Beijing. But being very poor and having no one to turn to, he soon decided to travel to the south to hide in the mountains. After a journey long and fraught with difficulties, he finally reached Mount Ermei in Szechuan Province. There he happened on two old Taoist masters named Gu Jici and Shang Daoyuan. They asked young Master Dong his reasons for coming to the mountains, and liking his character and bearing, decided to accept him as a disciple, teach him martial arts, and transmit the *He Luo Classic* [an ancient Daoist text].

The two venerable priests taught Master Dong a form of walking meditation that traversed a bagua circle. [See figure 3 on page 1.] They corrected his posture and movements and instructed him, saying, "Practice this technique while circling this tree until the tree begins to pursue you, then come report to us. You can feed yourself with food from the granaries and water from the stream." Master Dong was confused by their commands but did not dare to question them. He set about practicing as he was instructed and soon fell into a routine, thus setting his mind at ease. He trained long and hard for seven years until he had worn a path three feet deep around the tree. Then one day, while circling the tree, Master Dong suddenly observed the tree begin to tremble and lean in toward him, and he achieved sudden enlightenment. This was the fulfillment of the masters' prediction that the tree would "pursue" him.

He reported his breakthrough to his teachers, who congratulated him on his progress and praised him as a worthy student. They then instructed him in a method of circling two trees by walking in a figure eight. This young Master Dong did so for another two years until as before the trees "pursued" him. His teachers again lauded him for his steadfast progress and asked if he was homesick. Dong admitted that he was. On hearing this, his masters praised him for not losing his human nature. They then taught him "palm" changes and weapons forms for the next two years. After that, they pronounced his skills complete.

The two old Taoist sages then bade their student farewell and directed him to leave the mountain and return to his village. But first they instructed him that, as he passed through cities and towns on his journey, he was to call on the local martial arts schools and accept any challenges that came his way. Being a dutiful student, he did as he was told, competed with many boxers during his travels home, and was victorious over all comers. With each successful match, the fame of his skills and technique spread throughout the martial arts world.

When Master Dong finally returned to his village, he found his ancestral home abandoned and his parents long dead. It is indeed true that "the tree wishes to rest but the wind is unceasing; the child longs to support his parents, but they are gone." He mourned his parents, paid his last respects to his ancestors, and left his home for the capital in hopes of establishing himself there.

Having no place to stay in Beijing and very little money, Master Dong spent his days wandering about the Heaven's Bridge amusement district. In the evenings he slept in the open near Heaven's Altar, where the Emperor performed his annual rites on Lunar New Year. One day the martial arts teacher of a Manchu prince, Hou Zhenyuan, came to Heaven's Altar and happened to notice Master Dong. Despite his somewhat disheveled appearance, Hou observed the young man had a rugged countenance and flashing eyes. He could see that Dong was no ordinary person. After engaging him in conversation, and learning that he too was a martial artist, Hou asked him politely for a match of skills.

The two decided to use a straw mat, six by eight feet in size, as their ring; whoever stepped off the mat would be the loser. After Dong won three successive matches, Hou respectfully admitted defeat. However, he was so impressed with Master Dong that he subsequently found him a position as a servant in the palace in hopes of him someday instructing the prince.

The prince had no knowledge of Master Dong's skills. In fact, he himself was quite proficient in martial arts, practicing daily with great fervor, and had a very high opinion of his own skill. One day while the prince was working out, Master Dong made a small comment about his technique. When the prince heard this, he was quite surprised and ordered Master Dong to demonstrate his own skill before the assembled court. Master Dong's performance so amazed the prince that he realized at once that he was in the company of a true master. Without hesitation the prince asked Dong to take him on as a student. From that time forward, Master Dong's fame spread throughout the capital.

Alas it is said, "A tall tree catches too much wind, and fame attracts envy." Master Dong soon became a magnet for every boxer within a thousand miles who wanted to test his skills against the prince's new teacher. But they all went away with their feathers plucked. Many of these braggadocios exited the palace with stolen treasures and antiques, leaving behind messages daring Master Dong to come and get them. Dong traveled far and wide to retrieve the items in martial contests. Still the challenges and thievery continued over the course of many years, and Master Dong found little rest. Finally, Dong himself was implicated in some sort of criminal activity, and, in punishment, was castrated. From that time forward, the other servants in the palace referred to him as "Old Eunuch" instead of by his name.

As Master Dong grew older, he began to feel the art taught to him by his venerable teachers should be passed on to the next generation. He became acquainted with an eyeglass seller who often came to the palace to repair spectacles. His name was Cheng Tinghua. Master Dong was so impressed by Cheng's sincerity that he allowed him to become his first pupil from outside the palace gates. As the years passed, he took on more and more students from Beijing's common society. Thus over the years the fame of Bagua Zhang has spread until it has come to rival that of Taiji Quan and Xingyi Quan as one of the three great schools of "internal" martial arts.

When Master Dong passed away at age ninety, his students erected a mausoleum in his memory outside the West Gate of the capital. Each year, succeeding generations of his students still gather there to perform memorial rites in his honor. Although this grand master of a generation is gone, along with other great masters who followed in his steps, his art endures. However, the great social changes of our times have placed his great art in jeopardy of someday fading away from neglect. How sad!

The story of Dong Haiquan found in the Author's Foreword is one that was popular in Wang Shujin's native city of Tianjin around the time he was a young man studying martial arts. Variations of the story were also circulated in pulp fiction and magazine articles of the time. But how accurate is the account?

Modern scholarship has brought a more critical eye to bear on both Dong's life and the development of Bagua Zhang. Through extensive historical research a great many new details have been brought to light that constitute a verifiable record of Dong's connection with the emergence and popularization of Bagua Zhang.

If we look at the facts concerning Dong Haiquan's long and eventful life, they are startlingly brief. He was born in 1813 in Jujia Wu Township, Wenan County, Hebei Province. He began teaching martial arts openly in Beijing in 1870. He died in 1882 at the age of sixty-nine. All of this is a matter of public record. But a great deal more has been discovered about Dong's life from researching both palace and local records, sifting through the literature of the times, and interviewing descendents from Dong's home village.

Dong Haiquan was reported to have been a skilled martial artist as a young man growing up in Jujia Wu. It is not known for certain which styles he studied in his youth, although the types of martial arts most popular in and around his village were known to be Bafan Quan, Hung Quan, Hsing Men, and Jingong Quan. It is known, however, that around 1853 Dong Haiquan left his home in Wenan County and went to live with his cousins in nearby Kaiko County. His older cousin Dong Xianzhou was reputed to have been a skilled practitioner of Bafan Quan, and Dong Haiquan may have learned the style from him. This is of interest because Bafan Quan is a Northern Shaolin style that is unique in its use of open-palm strikes and other techniques that are found in present-day Bagua Zhang.

When Dong Haiquan left Kaiko he ventured south, traveling through several provinces and spending a good deal of time in the mountains. Exactly where he wandered, and what he did, is mostly a matter of conjecture. One thing known for certain is that somewhere along the line, he joined a sect of Daoism called Quan Zhen (Complete Truth/Reality). Quan Zhen Dao was part of the Lung Men (Dragon Gate) school of Daoism that was established by Zhou Zhangquan. Zhou was credited with developing a method of walking meditation that traversed a circle, often pacing around a tree. The Quan Zhen sect also practiced this type of meditation by walking a particular pattern, like the yin-yang symbol or a figure eight, while chanting a mantra. The reasoning behind the practice was to help calm the mind and eventually realize stillness in motion—both considered precursors to achieving a transcendental state of grace, or enlightenment.

The next known whereabouts of Dong Haiquan was when he surfaced in Beijing as a man of middle age. The stories of his escapades in the city are numerous and varied, but facts are limited. It is known, for example, that he was involved in some way with instructing guards and other personnel in the Imperial Palace. There are many tales told of his exploits there, but again most are apocryphal and undocumented. It is a matter of fact, however, that Dong started teaching openly in Beijing around 1870, when he was in his fifties. He taught continuously until his death in 1882, twelve years later.

The memorial stone, or stela, placed at Dong Haiquan's grave in 1883 lists a group of sixty-six students and/or admirers who were associated with him during his life. Among those names is found a group of students who were referred to as the "eight great" disciples. Their names are: Yin Fu, Cheng Tinghua, Sung Changrong, Ma Guei, Liu Dekuan, Liu Fengchun, Ma Weiqi, and Zhang Zhaodong. Several of these disciples became respected teachers in their own right and passed the art along to many students. Dong's two senior students, Yin Fu and Cheng Tinghua, have their names associated with two styles of Bagua Zhang that are still thriving today. The last named, Zhang Zhaodong, opened a martial arts school in Tianjin where Wang Shujin studied for eight years.

There were, of course, a great many other students who learned from Dong Haiquan or at least studied at his school. Some sources have placed that number in the hundreds. Many of these devotees went on to found their own schools and produce students who in turn became famous instructors themselves.

There are other elements of Wang Shujin's retelling of the Dong Haiquan legend that cannot be corroborated. One is the story of Dong learning Bagua Zhang from two mysterious Daoist adepts; the other is the tale of Dong becoming a eunuch through forced castration.

The story of Dong Haiquan being taught Bagua Zhang as a fully developed martial art by two mountain-dwelling Daoist recluses has all of the basic elements of many a martial arts legend in China. All you need to do is change the names and a few circumstances and you have Zhang Sanfeng creating Taiji Quan from a dream or Shaolin priests learning their art from an Indian monk. The Chinese love to shroud their origin myths in the mists of antiquity. It lends them a certain air of distinction and provides an unassailable historical precedent.

There are several elements of this legend that do not stand up well in the face of modern research. First, there has been no discoverable trace in history or literature of two Daoists named Gu Jici and Shang Daoyuan in the Mount Ermei region of Szechuan Province. Researchers who combed those fabled mountains interviewing present-day Daoist adepts found no temple records containing either name, nor of any Daoist recluses of that time who were known to teach martial arts. Second, facts point to Dong learning martial arts in his youth in Hebei Province that contained many elements found in modern Bagua Zhang. Third, Dong was a member of the Quan Zhen sect of Daoism and learned a method of walking meditation that resembles Bagua Zhang circle-walking patterns and steps. Finally, Dong Haiquan seemed quite happy to allow the origins of Bagua Zhang to be obscured by legend rather than have contemporaries believe that he had synthesized it whole cloth from elemental skills derived from previous training.

The legend of Dong Haiquan becoming a eunuch is a bit more difficult to dismiss out of hand. This story has been retold by third- and fourth-generation practitioners of Bagua Zhang but not, significantly, by first-generation students. There is also no evidence in imperial or local court records of Dong's forced castration. Castration was known as a common punishment in Chinese history up through the Sui Dynasty, but it was rarely used in the Ming and Ching eras except in extreme cases.

There are several stories about how Dong Haiquan became known as a eunuch. According to the story on his tombstone, he pretended to be a eunuch in order to enter into service in the residence of a Manchu prince. Another such tale has him pretending to be a eunuch in order to assassinate the emperor, a plot which obviously failed. There is yet another story which has Dong actually undergoing the operation of his own volition in order to obtain employment in the palace. Finally, there is Wang Shujin's version that has Dong involuntarily castrated for some unspecified crime. With a decided lack of corroborating evidence, we are left with examining a few facts about eunuchs to see if they might fit the picture of a great martial artist like Dong Haiquan.

Eunuchs *(taijian)* were employed in the imperial palace as advisors and servants of the inner circle of the emperor, and especially as retainers for emperor's concubines and female relatives. They were trusted because of their inability to participate in sexual congress with the ladies of the court.

Eunuchs came to their calling voluntarily. Self-inflicted eunuchism is a condition involving the surgical removal of the penis, scrotum, and testes. This complete castration of the genitalia in young males blocked the production of testosterone and the onset of puberty. The lack of testosterone production left eunuchs with high-pitched voices, flaccid musculature, soft rounded bellies, a lack of facial and body hair, and somewhat feminine features. Eunuchs also tended to age prematurely, so a man of forty often looked like one of sixty. Eunuchs were easily identified by their unique appearance. They were also roundly despised by the general population and were often objects of derision and caricature.

No eunuchs in Chinese history were ever known to be soldiers, palace guards, or martial artists. Dong Haiquan, on the other hand, was described as an unusually strong and robust figure with the "back of a horse." His reputed great strength, agility, and athletic prowess would seem to fly in the face of accusations of his being a eunuch. There is also the matter of his great success in attracting some of Beijing's best young martial artists to his inner circle. It is difficult to see how a eunuch, universally reviled among the citizenry, could ever achieve such a feat.

The last question to take up in our quest for the real Dong Haiquan is whether he popularized an art that had existed previously or invented his own style by marrying disparate methodologies into one cohesive system. This issue is made more difficult when you consider that Dong, when asked by his disciples where he learned Bagua Zhang, would comment that he received his art from "a man who lived in the mountains."

If the system existed before Dong Haiquan, we know it was not called Bagua Zhang. That name was unknown before his time. In fact, Dong's first-generation students stated the original name for the system was Zhuan Zhang (Rotating Palms). Later it was expanded to Bagua Zhuan Zhang. Finally, probably near the end of Dong's life or perhaps even posthumously, it was shortened to Bagua Zhang.

Several martial systems predating Bagua Zhang have been examined as possible precursors to the art, but none contain all of the elements present in Dong's method.

Of course, you can take Bagua Zhang apart piece by piece and identify known techniques that existed before the art; but since there are only so many ways to move the human body, such similarities are to be expected. There are also certain styles of Bagua Zhang that claimed to have been established before Dong began teaching (some by many hundreds of years), but exhaustive investigation has ruled them out one by one as being wholly derived from Bagua Zhang and Dong Haiquan.

We can probably never say with absolute certainty if Dong Haiquan learned his art from another source and merely popularized it, or whether he synthesized techniques learned from several sources and created an entirely new martial system. In any event, Dong was certainly good at marketing his product and keeping the source, as he played his cards, very close to the vest. As Lao Tzu once said, "The sage wears rough clothing and embraces the jewel within."

*Figure 2: Master Dong Haiquan depicted in a portrait painted by one of his students*

# 1 An Explanation of Bagua Zhang and the Eight Trigrams of the Yi Jing

The illustration in figure 3 appears to be pedestrian but is actually profound. In its largest sense it embraces the universe; in its smallest it can encompass a person's body (figure 4). Cultivating Dao and enriching humanity is the essence of Bagua Zhang practice. If you do not grasp the true meaning of the elements within the illustration, even if you follow the instructions step-by-step and practice hard, your movements will be mechanical and you will not obtain true spiritual growth. Because of this, our teachers valued their art highly and did not transmit it lightly.

*Figure 3: Bagua diagram*

*Figure 4: Hands embrace the yin-yang fish; feet tread the bagua diagram*

The inner circle of the illustration represents the beginning of the concept of duality, commonly called the *taiji* form. The diagram uses the form of two fish swimming to represent taiji, the yin and yang. The taiji symbol is characterized in linear form by the *liang'yi*, or two intentions (figure 5). From liang'yi arises the *si'xiang*, or the four directions (figure 6). From the si'xiang arises *bagua*, or the eight trigrams. The bagua represent the basic forms of the natural world from which arise the myriad manifestations of our universe. The bagua can also be used to express the nature of divisions within the human body. In Bagua Zhang the head is represented by *qian*, the abdomen by *kun*, the kidneys by *kan*, the heart by *li*, the sacrum by *xun*, the neck by *gen*, the stomach by *zhen*, and the spleen by *dui*. It is said that Fu Xi created bagua to teach people to harmonize with the flow of yin and yang and to sort out the natural essence of all things in the world.

*Figure 5: Liang'yi, or two intentions*      *Figure 6: Si'xiang, or the four directions*

On the outer circle of the illustration there are eight terms: *tui, tuo, dai, ling, ban, kou, pi,* and *jin*. These are the eight major movement forms of Bagua Zhang. Each form matches with one of the bagua. The practice of each form should match with the essential character of each *gua*. To relate the symbols correctly we must understand the six rules or methods of creating Chinese calligraphy. In ancient times, before written language, people recorded events by using knotted cords. The markings of bagua were a more advanced method of recording things. Until Cang Jie created writing, people collected all manner of marks and forms to set down the six methods of creating words. The methods were:

> *xiangxin:* using the shapes of things
> *huiyi:* using the meanings of things
> *xingshen:* imitating the sounds of things
> *zishi:* pointing to symbols
> *chuanchu:* using the definitions of things
> *jiajie:* borrowing categories

These are the six categories under which Chinese characters are grouped. How Bagua Zhang matches with each trigram is by imitating a portion of the six methods of language creation by using shape, meaning, and borrowing of forms as in the following section.

Qian: This first trigram is composed of three unbroken lines, and thus is very yang in nature. The ancient interpretation is that good people should constantly improve themselves, like nature. The palm form is *tui*, or push. Your practice should be like the lines of the trigram—top to bottom, inside and out, with strong and unbroken Qi. Qian is the first trigram of the eight. It represents a new beginning. That is why the first form in Bagua Zhang (Single Palm Change) utilizes qian and the application of tui. If you practice the movements evenly from beginning to end, your blood flow will be smooth; if not, your heart will not open properly and the flow of blood will be blocked.

Kan: According to the trigram shape, the center is full, which means sinking inward. It also has the connotation of being dangerous. If you want to avoid danger, you need to have a strong will to survive. The palm form is called *tuo*, to hold up. When you practice tuo you should be like the trigram and be outwardly soft but strong within. Strengthen your heart by collecting your Qi. The hand form is smooth and flexible. In this book the fifth form (White Snake Spits Out Tongue) uses both the shape and energy of tuo. If you practice the form smoothly, it will elevate the fire in the heart and you will not become dizzy.

Gen: The trigram shape appears like an overturned bowl; the bottom is facing upward and the interior is concealed. The principle of movement is turning back and cutting off. The palm form is *dai*, to carry. The way to practice dai is to take on the form of gen itself, and be firm on the top and pliant beneath. Project the energy of stillness and repose. In this book the sixth form (Mighty Peng Spreads Wings) utilizes dai in structure and intention. If practiced well, the heart's Qi will descend and spread to the four limbs.

Zhen: The trigram shape is symbolized by a basin standing upright. The principle is one of vibrating or quaking. Powerful actions bring fearful reactions that will lead to order and control. The awe of power opens the way. The palm form is *ling,* to lead. In practice ling emulates the form of zhen, yielding above but firm below; seeking stillness within movement. This is the birth of yang. The intention is one of searching deeply and unpredictable change. The third form (Hawk Swoops Upward) utilizes the technique of ling as its theme. If practiced correctly, the liver's Qi will be harmonized; if not you will become easily angered.

Xun: The trigram is broken on the bottom. Xun means to enter like the wind. There is no opening so small the wind cannot penetrate. The palm form is *ban,* to move about. The way to practice xun is to have firm intent in the middle and upper body while keeping your footwork mobile. The technique is one of carrying. The eighth form (Whirlwind Palms) employs ban as its main action. If practiced smoothly, your Qi will spread to the four limbs and your body will move like a windmill in a gale.

Li: The composition of the trigram is empty in the center. Li means to adhere to. The palm form is *kou,* to button or hook. The way to practice kou is to be pliant within and resolute without. Remain flexible in the center like a snake wriggling through a small opening. The second form (Double Palm Change) employs the use of kou to penetrate. If practiced smoothly, your mind will melt into emptiness.

Kun: The trigram is composed of three lines broken into six parts. The ancient meaning of kun arises from the purity of a female horse. A mare is very mild and composed yet capable of swift and sudden flight. The palm form is *pi,* to split. The way to perform pi is to have both top and bottom and interior and exterior in harmony. The fourth form (Yellow Dragon Rolls Over) and sixth form (Mighty Peng Spreads Wings) use pi as their major actions. If practiced smoothly, your movements will be light and quick.

Dui: The trigram is broken on top. Dui is symbolized by a swamp where water gathers. Here it represents something more like a pond. The palm form is *jin,* to enter. In practice dui is soft and supple on top and firm and strong below. The form is contracted like a crouching tiger ready to spring forward. The seventh form

(White Ape Presents Peaches) employs jin. If the movements are practiced smoothly, your lung Qi will be pure and fluid; if not, your Qi will not be harmonized and it may lead to asthmatic wheezing.

The definitions above are just rough explanations of a much larger picture. As for the details, it depends on the learner to study, question, consider, analyze, and practice in order to find deeper meaning. The eight forms should also be examined and practiced individually. In conclusion, the more diligently you study, the greater your return. Bagua Zhang forms imitate the nature of heaven and earth. Follow the principles of yin-yang and harmonize with the seasons, and you will benefit humanity by developing a more universal view of life. Embracing the yin-yang fish and treading the bagua diagram, you will walk the circle as though striding through the cosmos.

## *"Bagua Linked Palms" Chart of Associations*

| Trigram | Name | Palm Change | Palm Form | Action | Body Part | Nature Reference |
|---|---|---|---|---|---|---|
| ䷀ | 乾 Qian | Single Palm Change | Cutting | Pushing *tui* | Head | Tiger |
| ䷜ | 坎 Kan | White Snake Spits Out Tongue | Lifting | Lifting *tuo* | Kidneys | Snake |
| ䷳ | 艮 Gen | Mighty Peng Spreads Wings | Carrying | Carrying *dai* | Neck | Peng (Giant Roc) |
| ䷲ | 震 Zhen | Hawk Swoops Upward | Grasping | Leading *ling* | Stomach | Hawk |
| ䷸ | 巽 Xun | Whirlwind Palms | Supporting | Move about *ban* | Sacrum | Wind |
| ䷝ | 離 Li | Double Palm Change | Piercing | Hooking *kou* | Heart | Snake |
| ䷁ | 坤 Kun | Yellow Dragon Rolls Over | Thrusting | Splitting *pi* | Abdomen | Dragon |
| ䷹ | 兌 Dui | White Ape Presents Peaches | Penetrating | Entering *jin* | Spleen | Monkey |

CHAPTER

2 The Eight Secrets of Bagua Zhang

The forms of Bagua Zhang and Xingyi Quan look different in practice, but the principles are congruent throughout. When practicing Bagua Zhang, use the principles of Xingyi Quan to build power and cultivate Qi to the highest level. As Meng Zi said, "to cultivate my magnificent Qi." The "Qi" Meng Zi was referring to is the true Qi that fills the void between heaven and earth. Here are the Eight Secrets of Bagua Zhang:

1.  Three *Ding* [highest, outermost point]: The head floats upward; the palms press outward; the tongue ascends. Flatten the back of the head and push the crown upward like a power rushing toward the sky. The head is the master of the body when it is pointing heavenward, allowing the three major acupuncture points on the spine to flow freely: the *yuzhen* point, behind the head; the *lulu* point, between the shoulder blades; and the *weilu* point, near the base of the spine. Then the kidney Qi will reach to the *niwan* point between the eyebrows to discipline the temperament. Palms press outward with an expression of power like pushing a mountain. Then Qi will flow through the body, and power will expand to the four limbs. The tongue pressing upward to the roof of the mouth will guide rising kidney Qi downward to the *dantian* to solidify the life force.

2.  Three *Kou* [clamp, compress]: Shoulders clamp inward; backs of the hands and tops of the feet compress; teeth set. When the back clamps inward, the chest will hollow and Qi power will fill your internal organs. When the hands and feet are compressed, Qi will flow to the arms, and your step will be steady and powerful. When you set the teeth, your tendons and bones will compress.

3.  Three *Yuan* [round, wrap]: Round the back and spine; round the chest; wrap the tiger's mouth [a shape made by the angle between the thumb and forefinger when forming the Vertical Palm; see chapter 5]. Round the back,

= 7 =

and spine and power will fill the body. Straighten the coccyx, and your spirit will flow upward. Round the chest inward, and power will extend to your elbows; the upper abdomen contracts slightly and the breath flows easily. Round the tiger's mouth, and a great power will flow outward; your hands will have an outwardly stretched and inwardly wrapping strength.

4. Three *Min* [alert, sensitive, quick]: The mind is alert; the eyes sensitive; the hands quick. When the mind is alert you can react quickly to change. When the eyes remain sensitive you can anticipate openings. When the hands are agile you can take the initiative before the opponent can enter.

5. Three *Bao* [embrace, hold]: The dantian embraces; the heart holds; the ribs encompass. The dantian embraces Qi to keep it from scattering, allowing you to attack the enemy. The heartbeat holds steady, so you will not panic upon meeting your foe. The rib cage protects the internal organs, so you face the adversary without danger.

6. Three *Chui* [hang down, drop]: Qi descends; shoulders drop; elbows hang. When Qi descends to the dantian, your body will be as steady as a mountain. Drop the shoulders and the arms will elongate and become more lively, and the shoulders will lead the elbows. Hang the elbows and the forearms will round naturally, strengthening the muscles of the chest.

7. Three *Qu* [bend, curve]: Arms curve; knees bend; wrists bow. When arms curve like a half moon, your strength will be abundant. When knees bend like a half moon, your power will be substantial. When wrists bow like a half moon, your power will be concentrated. The natural stretch and contraction of the joints produces a bouncy unbroken strength.

8. Three *Ting* [straighten, pull up]: Pull up the neck and flatten the head, and Qi will flow to the crown. Lengthen the spine and flatten the lower back, and power will reach to the tips of the four limbs, and Qi will fill your entire body. Pull up the knee caps, and your Qi will be tranquil and your spirit harmonious, like a tree growing roots.

CHAPTER

3 Explanation of Bagua Zhang's Nine Palaces
Returning to One

When you practice Bagua Zhang, besides understanding body movement in relation to the nature of the art, you also need to pay attention to the coordination of your own body. This will help to collect power in your body and concentrate it at one point. Use this point to hit a target, and the result will be incredible power. This kind of effect in turn is called Nine Palaces Retuning to One.

To understand the rule of the Nine Palaces you need to understand the meaning of the Nine Palaces in relation to the bagua of our own bodies:

1. Dantian is the root, heart is the middle, head is the tip.
2. Shoulders are the root, elbows are the middle, hands are the tips.
3. Hips are the root, knees are the middle, feet are the tips.

Altogether there are nine segments that are called the Nine Palaces: trunk, shoulders, arms, hands, fingers, buttocks, thighs, feet, and tongue. Altogether there are nine parts, which corresponds to the *Luo Shu* text. After you gain an understanding of Nine Palaces, you need to pay attention to the three basins:

1. The head is the heavenly basin. It appears to be lifting heroically to heaven, so you can uplift your spirit and concentrate your mind.
2. The body is the middle basin. Get rid of the bad habits of leaning forward, backward, or to the right or left; then the nervous system can respond quickly and Qi will flow freely.
3. Stepping methods represent the earth basin: Inch Step [*Cun Bu*], Sinking Step [*Dian Bu*], Swinging Step [*Bai Bu*], Hooking Step [*Kou Bu*], Scissor Step [*Jian Bu*], and Continuous Step [*Gua Bu*] all have to be done correctly.

You have to understand the three segments. The hands are the tip of the segment. If the tip is not understood, you will lose its guidance and falter in your intent. The body is the middle segment. If it is not understood, the body will become empty. The feet are the root segment. If the root itself is not clear, you will become unbalanced and stumble. The three segments must have clarity of purpose in both stillness and movement. In order to comprehend the movements of the three segments, you must follow the strictures of the Eight Secrets of Bagua Zhang. If they are not understood, you will surely miss the point.

These three basins and segments are ruled by the *yi* (will). As the Confucians say: One to rule them all. The meaning is that the three segments must form continuous unbroken movement from beginning to end. If they do, from your head to your feet, the three segments unite as one. There will be no hesitation or broken movement; your strength will be drawn together as one. This is the power of the Nine Palaces Returning to One.

# 4 Bagua Zhang Post Standing Methods

Z han Zhuang [Post Standing] is the most fundamental skill of martial arts practice. The more you stand, the more stable your foundation will be. Bagua Zhang Post Standing is called Primordial or Universal Standing. Types of Post Standing postures include:

- Horse Stance
- Figure Eight Stance
- Crouching Tiger Stance
- T-Shape Stance
- Bow and Arrow Stance
- Single Leg Stance

This is a very short and somewhat cryptic section of the text that offers no photos, illustrations, or descriptions to guide the reader in what was a very important part of Wang Shujin's martial arts curriculum. Zhan Zhuang literally means "standing on posts/pilings" (driven into the ground). It is a type of rooting training in which the practitioner stands still in a variety of postures to develop a kind of whole-body integrity. It is a derivation of Shaolin-type stance training, in which practitioners would strengthen their legs and improve balance by stepping on wooden pilings of varying heights.

Wang Shujin's Post Standing is practiced while standing in place on a flat surface. This type of training arose in part from standing and walking meditation methods of Daoist monks. Xingyi Quan also has a similar practice called San Ti, or stance keeping. In fact, there is an entire quasi-martial discipline, called Yi Quan, which is devoted to various standing meditation methods. Wang Shujin was taught Yi Quan by its founder, Wang Xiangzhai.

Post Standing does not, however, appear to be a universal practice in other Bagua Zhang styles. Wang Shujin had his students stand in the postures at the beginning of each practice session regardless of whether he was teaching Taiji Quan, Xingyi Quan, or Bagua Zhang.

Wang introduced other post-standing postures, with accompanying photos, in his second book, *Bagua Swimming Body Palms*. The postures shown here were photographed, interestingly enough, in Japan on the roof of the Diet (parliament) building in Tokyo in the 1960s.

*Bodhidharma Stance (Da Mo Zhuang)*

*Double Separation Stance (Shuang Fen Zhuang)*

*Double Push Stance (Shuang Tui Zhuang)*

*Double Ward-Off Stance (Shuang Peng Zhuang)*

*Joyful Stance (Huan Xi Zhuang)*

*Crouching Tiger Stance (Hu Zuo Zhuang)*

*Smooth Step Single Ward-Off Stance (Shun Bu Dan Peng Zhuang)*

*Smooth Step Double Ward-Off Stance (Shun Bu Shuang Peng Zhuang)*

# 5 An Explanation of Bagua Zhang Hand Forms

**Vertical Palm [Li Zhang]**
The thumb is held horizontally, the index finger is straight, the middle and ring fingers are slightly curved, and the little finger is level. The center of the palm is made empty. When the elbow is dropped, the hand forms the shape of a lotus leaf. The palm, wrist, and elbow exhibit an outwardly stretched, inwardly wrapped type of strength.

*Vertical Palm*

**Piercing Palm [Zuan Zhang]**
The center of the palm faces upward, and the edge faces inward. The piercing movement implies a twisting strength.

*Piercing Palm*

**Carrying Palm [Tuo Zhang]**
The palm faces forward [fingers downward] as if pushing something.

*Carrying Palm*

**Splitting Palm [Pi Zhang]**
The palm is held vertically with the fingertips pointing forward and the palm edge downward. The palm falls in one smooth motion.

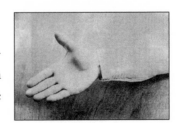
*Splitting Palm*

*Scooping Palm*

### Scooping Palm [Liao Zhang]

The palm may face inward or outward. From a lower position it scoops upward and away.

*Cow's Tongue Palm*

### Cow's Tongue Palm [Niushi Zhang]

The fingertips clinch together forming a shape like a cow's tongue.

*Lifting Palm*

### Lifting Palm [Tiao Zhang]

The palm lifts upward or forward with the fingers pointing upward.

*Slicing Palm*

### Slicing Palm [Qie Zhang]

The palm faces downward and uses a slicing or shaving motion. It also has a feeling of splitting.

## All Parts of the Hand May Be Used

- The fingertips can poke
- The knuckles and backs of the hands can strike
- The palms can slap
- The palm edges can chop or push
- The base of the palm can press
- The wrists and elbows can bump or smash

CHAPTER

# 6 The Thirteen Prohibitions

1. Don't indulge excessively in sensual pleasures.

2. Don't practice when you are distraught or ill at ease.

3. Don't practice in stagnant or polluted air.

4. Don't practice when it's windy; practice standing meditation in calm conditions.

5. Don't practice on a full stomach or eat or smoke directly afterward.

6. Don't become out of breath or use excessive force during practice.

7. Don't wear wet clothing in the wind after practice; change immediately.

8. Don't sit down directly after practice; walk slowly for ten minutes.

9. Don't go to the toilet or talk right after practice.

10. Don't practice when fatigued.

11. Don't drink to excess or take stimulants.

12. Don't skip training levels.

13. Don't become arrogant or disdainful of others.

# 7 Basic Principles

**E**mpty Spirit, Raise Energy: Keep the head erect and straighten the back of the neck. The back of the head should float upward, but it should be held naturally. Keep your gaze level.

**Contain Chest, Pull up Back:** Keep the upper body erect. Do not pull up the chest. Wrap the shoulders inward and round the back. The chest is held comfortably; Qi should flow easily.

**Draw Together Lower Abdomen:** The dantian is a good place to accumulate Qi. Keep the lower abdomen empty so Qi can sink. This is not achieved by hollowing the abdomen but by turning the upper thighs slightly inward and dropping the coccyx, which draws the area in and down. This is also called embracing the belly.

**Breathe Slowly and Gradually:** Breathe through the nose; do not use the mouth. The breath must be slow and even like a cloud floating in the sky.

**Coccyx Upright:** From the neck to the tip of the coccyx you must be extended and erect. This will allow the spinal nerves to function normally during exercise, and your reflexes will be unimpeded and lively.

**Draw in Buttocks, Pull up Sphincter:** Relax the lower back from the waist to the coccyx. The coccyx will naturally tuck inward as the buttocks are drawn down. You should have the intention of lightly contracting the area between the anus and the genitals.

**Sink Shoulders, Drop Elbows:** The shoulders have the feeling of being almost dislocated. The elbows hang downward as if weighted. Only if the elbows hang will the shoulders be able to sink. In this way Qi will be allowed to penetrate to the fingers.

**Tongue Touches Roof of Mouth:** The tip of the tongue touches the roof of the mouth between the upper teeth and the hard palate. Close the mouth lightly and touch the teeth together. The tongue-to-palate bridge connection allows Qi to flow without blockage. Pressing too hard with the tongue, clenching the teeth, or closing the mouth too tightly will blunt Qi.

**The Six Unities:** Mind and yi (intention), yi and Qi, Qi and *li* (muscular strength), hands and feet, shoulders and hips. Only when these six points are united and harmonious will your movements be connected as one.

**Yi is Commander in Chief:** Movements of internal martial arts are arrived at through the mind, and Bagua Zhang is no exception. Internal energy and external strength must act as one with one intent. In movement seek stillness.

**Legs Bent, Treading in Mud:** This describes Bagua Zhang circle walking. The walking is smooth and flowing. This is a special characteristic of Bagua Zhang. Do not walk upright; sit with both legs bent. As you step forward, keep the foot close to the ground. The toes should grip lightly, which will cause the sole of the foot to hollow. Step as if walking through mud. The heel and instep touch the ground at the same time. In this way, your weight will be centered. After lengthy practice your step will be light and quick like flowing water. As you step forward the foot touches down lightly; the back foot is kept flat with a slight intention of stepping up on something. As you step forward the ankles brush and the foot hooks inward as it is placed down.

**Waist Acts as Axis:** Bagua Zhang uses rotation of the waist to lead the four limbs. The upper body initiates arm movement; the waist drives the upper body.

**Spread Fingers, Hollow Palms:** The fingers spread apart, the thumb is held level, the index finger is held upright, and the other three fingers curl inward. The thumbs and little fingers form triangles; the palms hollow naturally. This is called the lotus-leaf palm.

# 8 Bagua Zhang Linked Palms Form

## Preparation

1. Take one large step out from center and use it as the radius of your circle. The line of the circle, one foot wide, will be the orbit for practice.
2. Your feet should straddle the line of the circle shoulders' width apart and parallel to each other. Face the east with the left shoulder toward the center of the circle. Your shoulders and hands hang naturally, and the palms face the legs. Straighten up the body, and focus the eyes on the tip of the nose (just like the Basic Principles of Bagua Zhang, 1 through 8). Empty your mind of any conscious thoughts. You should have only a tiny flow of Qi in your abdomen. This is called the *wuji* [infinity] posture (figure 13).

*Figure 13*

# First Palm Form: "Single Palm Change"

Starting from the wuji posture, your mind makes the slightest intention of movement, which is called the beginning of Taiji.

1. Use waist power to sink down, bending your legs slowly, and sit in your stance. Do not let your knees extend beyond your toes. Beginners may stand in a higher posture and bend lower later on.
2. Twist your waist right, leading your shoulders to the right side. Move the right heel 30 degrees toward the left foot. Weight the right foot and empty the left.
3. The two palms follow the shoulder turn to the right, then follow the waist as it twists to the left toward the right front. Palms face upward as high as your head as if holding something. This is called Right Ward-Off [peng] (figure 14).
4. Continue this movement toward the upper left until you form Left Ward-Off.
5. As you perform Left Ward-Off, your weight transfers to the left foot, emptying the right. Your waist twists to the right, and the right foot steps out, adding weight, but your hands do not move from Left Ward-Off position. Lift up your left foot and extend it toward the right side of the circle. The thigh is held horizontally to the floor, the shin hangs vertically, and the toes point downward. The waist twists, and you shift weight onto your hip. Your head and shoulders stay twisted to the left, and your eyes look at the tip of the left index finger.

*Figure 14*

*Figure 15*

At this point, your arm and shoulder are held at a 90-degree angle to your trunk; the left palm and right foot should form a 180-degree angle. Your entire body should be rooted and steady (figure 15).

6. Place your left foot down inside the line of the circle. Take a step, big or small depending on your body size, but it should be natural and balanced. Shift your weight to the left foot. Step forward with the right foot to the outside of the circle, brushing the left ankle as you go; when you step downward, your toes turn slightly inward to conform with the line of the circle. The angle of the feet forms a triangle shape. As you walk, your palms continuously adjust to the curve of the circle. Your left wrist twists outward until the second knuckle of your little finger and index finger point toward the center of the circle. The tip of the index finger is held level with your eyes. Your palm stands straight and twists outward; the arms are bent like a half moon. The right palm faces downward, and your thumb points toward your navel. You "sit" your wrist and your arm, and the palms feel externally stretched and inwardly wrapped.

*Figure 16*

Drop your elbows; relax your shoulders. While you are walking, your left arm projects its power toward the center of the circle and not to the front (figure 16). The posture is like two hands embracing the yin-yang fish and the feet treading on the bagua diagram. It matches the shape of the Taiji symbol. That is why Bagua Zhang has the shape of the Taiji symbol. Some people say it is a yin-yang form, because it emphasizes the division between yin and yang.

7. Changing Palms: The steps above were in preparation for the Single Palm Change. How many steps you take to traverse the circle is up to the length of your stride. In a formal performance you walk around the circle one and a half times. You are now prepared to begin the left Single Palm Change.

a. Hook your right foot inward, or *kou bu* (figure 17).

b. Using the ball of your left foot as the center of the movement, turn to the left 180 degrees until your body faces the rear. Twisting your right heel, take a half step forward with the left foot, hooking the toe inward slightly as you step down. The left palm turns downward and is held at shoulder height. The left thumb points to your right heel. The arm forms a half circle, and from palm to shoulder there is a feeling of being outwardly stretched and internally wrapped. The right palm turns upward and is held near the right abdomen. Sink into the *kua* [juncture of the hip and thigh]. The right kua and foot form a straight line. Seventy percent of your weight is on the right foot. This posture is called Crouching Tiger (figure 18).

c. From the Crouching Tiger posture, the toe of the front foot turns outward, and you twist the waist to the right and shift weight onto the front leg. The forward hand does not change position but follows the body turn. The right hand drills forward under the left arm. The head turns to watch the left hand. Slide the now unweighted right foot forward, brushing the knees together. You should be balanced and stable. Twist your waist to the right as you lift your left leg up toward the outside of the circle. Sink into your left kua (figure 19). Perform the Right Ward-Off movement, keeping your gaze fixed on the right index finger.

d. End the form by setting your right foot down and stepping forward with the left. Continue walking the circle on the right side [left shoulder toward the circle] in the same manner you did on the left, constantly adjusting your palms to the center of the circle as you go.

8. As you turn, lift up the left leg and stretch it toward the outside of the circle. Twist the waist and stabilize your balance. Place the left foot down parallel with the right, about shoulders' width apart. Drop your hands as in preparation to begin.

*Figure 17*　　　　　*Figure 18*　　　　　*Figure 19*

Explanation:

1. All the previous step-by-step instructions require clear understanding. When you practice, the four directions have to be continuously linked.

2. There is yin and yang within the movements. There is substantial and insubstantial. There is internal and external. They seem to conflict. But actually it is Bagua Zhang's purpose to use positive and negative to create a new type of power. When there is antagonism, your muscles contract and issue forth this power.

3. From Right Ward-Off to Left Ward-Off, your arms turn like wheels; this is called *gun* [rolling]. The rolling movement includes both twisting and turning, just like the power of turning a screwdriver; this is called *zuan* [drilling]. These two complex movements create the great power that is required by Bagua Zhang.

4. The Crouching Tiger is a form of stance training. As you perform it you should slow your movements and modulate your breathing.

*Figure 1-1*

*Figure 1-2*

*Figure 1-3*

*Figure 1-4*

*Figure 1-5*

*Figure 1-6*

Figure 1-7               Figure 1-8               Figure 1-9

Figure 1-10               Figure 1-11

Figure 1-12

Figure 1-13

Figure 1-14

Figure 1-15

Figure 1-16

Figure 1-17

*Figure 1-18*

*Figure 1-19*

*Single Palm Change in defense*

Single Palm Change holds the key to all basic movements and body principles of the Bagua Zhang form. All styles of Bagua Zhang have a version of the Single Palm Change. It is nearly always represented by the qian trigram. Qian, with its three unbroken lines, is considered pure yang in character. The principle movement of the form, Crouching Tiger, is performed in a very forceful yang manner. Wang Shujin linked the trigram shapes to the structure of the human body. Three solid lines represent unbroken strength in the upper (head, arms, and trunk), middle (waist and hips), and lower (legs and feet) sections of the body.

The Crouching Tiger is a straightforward, slightly angled movement that can attack with the slicing palm or hit with any area of the body from the shoulder to the thighs. The action is called tui, or push. Wang Shujin said that if it is done smoothly, the form will promote good circulation throughout the body. If performed improperly, the action can harm the heart.

Yi Jing Connection: Qian represents heaven. The way of heaven is turning and changing constantly without ceasing—like an energetic dragon soaring in the sky. Qian is the spirit of yang and projects pure energy and motion. As a human attribute it is to be strong and diligent. The opposite of qian is kun.

# Second Palm Form: "Double Palm Change"

1. As you walk the circle on the right side [left shoulder inward], turn in toward the center of the circle making a hooking step, or kou bu, with the right foot. Then turn left and step out to Crouching Tiger (figure 20).

*Figure 20*

2. Turn the toes of the left foot outward and take a long arching step forward with the right foot. At the same time, the right palm shoots out forward from under the mouth and over the back of the left hand, and pierces upward and outward with a drilling strength. The left palm is held below the right elbow (figure 21).

*Figure 21*

3. From the last position, twist the waist toward the left, pivoting the right foot inward, so both feet form a figure resembling the (Chinese) number 8 (/\). Simultaneously twist your right palm inward, raising the arm slightly to cover the head. The left palm turns over to face upward, and the fingers twist inward to point toward the side of the chest. Shift your weight onto the right hip, bend both knees, and slowly lower your posture (figure 22).

Twist the waist and neck toward the left rear as you sink lower. Lift your left foot off the floor and brush past your right ankle as you take a long step to the rear. Sit low and light on the right hip, keeping the upper body straight, just like the Taiji Quan "Snake Descends the Tree" movement (figure 23). Within the same movement, the left arm follows the turn of the waist [twisting, dropping, and drilling] as it passes under the left armpit, moving past the left hip, and shoots toward the left foot. The left elbow faces upward; this is called leading *[ling]*. As the left hand moves, the right palm crosses the chest to a position, palm up, under the left armpit.

*Figure 22*          *Figure 23*

4. Continue the left waist movement by twisting the toes of your left foot outward and shifting your weight onto the forward leg. The left arm follows the movement of the body, twisting until the elbow faces downward. As you twist, the left palm pushes upward and outward. The right palm passes under the left arm and embraces your left shoulder. End the form by performing Right Ward-Off as in the Single Palm Change.

5. Perform the Double Palm Change on the left side by reversing right and left in the directions above.

### The Complete Sequence of Double Palm Change

*Figure 2-1*              *Figure 2-2*              *Figure 2-3*

Figure 2-4

Figure 2-5

Figure 2-6

Figure 2-7

Figure 2-8

Figure 2-9

*Figure 2-10*

*Figure 2-11*

*Figure 2-12*

*Figure 2-13*

Double Palm Change is represented by the li trigram and is also found within every orthodox Bagua Zhang style. Wang Shujin's Double Palm Change begins with the cutting palm, as does Single Palm Change, then moves inward to apply the piercing palm. The li trigram suggests the third movement of the change, in which the practitioner spins to the rear while his hand drills through the middle and down the leg. Wang likened this move to a snake wriggling through a hole.

To perform the movement properly, one must be externally firm while remaining internally soft and flowing. This is the physical embodiment of li with the strength of yang above and below and the fluid nature of yin in the center. The action involved is kou, or hooking inward. Both Wang Shujin and Sun Lutang made the same cryptic observation that if Double Palm Change is performed correctly, "the heart will remain empty." Whether this refers to the organ itself or the internal center of the body is unclear.

Yi Jing Connection: Li is symbolized by fire and is clear and fluid. It is abstract and has no defined shape: You can only feel its Qi. Fire clings to other objects and depends on them to manifest itself. A yin line develops between two yang lines, meaning to lean on or depend on. There is a feeling of flowing through space and rushing upward. The opposite of li is kan. Kan stands for power locked within, and li for radiance and expansion.

# Third Palm Form: "Hawk Swoops Upward"

1. As you walk the circle on the right side, turn in toward the center by making a hooking step, or kou bu, with the right foot. The left foot then arcs around 180 degrees, and the right follows and sets down parallel to the left foot. At the same time, the right palm turns inward, moves forward past the chest, and twists toward the face as it shoots straight upward; keep the arm bent like a half moon. Simultaneously, the left palm moves down outside the right arm and presses downward with the palm facing the floor. The upper and lower body remain upright and natural (figure 24).

*Figure 24*

2. Continuing from above, and moving from the center of the hands and feet, twist the waist to the left, turning the neck leftward, and shift your weight onto the right hip (figure 25). Next, lower your body while lifting the left foot off the ground. Brush the left foot by the right ankle as you take a long step to the rear, performing "Snake Creeps Down." The palms turn down, with an outwardly stretched and inwardly wrapped power, and both strike outward. The left palm descends toward the left foot, keeping very low; the right palm chops upward and to the right. The lower your stance, the better; of course, the height depends on your strength and balance. Both arms remain bent like two half moons (figure 26).

*Figure 25*     *Figure 26*

3. To finish the form, turn the toes of the left foot outward in a swing step, or Bai Bu, while the left palm pushes, twists, and lifts. Bring the right foot forward to rest next to the left. Shoot the right palm under the left shoulder and perform Right Ward-Off as in the Double Palm Change.

4. Perform Hawk Swoops Upward on the left side by reversing right and left in the directions above.

## The Complete Sequence of Hawk Swoops Upward

Figure 3-1

Figure 3-2

Figure 3-3

Figure 3-4

Figure 3-5

Figure 3-5 (side view)

Figure 3-6

Figure 3-6 (rear view)

Figure 3-7

Figure 3-8

Figure 3-9

Figure 3-10

*Figure 3-11*

*Figure 3-12*

*Figure 3-13*

Hawk Swoops Upward is the third palm change in Wang Shujin's basic form and is represented by the zhen trigram. In other styles this palm change is sometimes called Swallow Skims Water. The hawk swoops down close to the ground and then soars up high in a long arcing movement. This mimics a raptor pouncing on its prey (or a swallow skimming a pond for a drink). The palm form is grasping. The action is ling, or leading. The practitioner engages the opponent and leads him in a circle ending in a lock, spinning throw, or take-down.

The softer, flowing movements of the upper body are supported by the strong and balanced stepping below. You can see this structure clearly in the zhen trigram with yin on top held up by yang below. The key to the Hawk's martial power is being externally hard while keeping internally active. Wang Shujin said if you execute the form correctly, the liver's Qi will be in harmony.

Yi Jing Connection: Zhen is represented by thunder. It embodies movement, being proactive, and keeping alert. Overcome external power by not resisting and staying in the center of motion. The movement is quick like thunder and causes fright (the startle reflex). Stay still until your composure returns. This echoes Wang's dictum of stillness within movement.

# Fourth Palm Form: "Yellow Dragon Rolls Over"

1. As you walk the circle on the right side, the right foot steps forward, angling away toward the outside of the circle. The feet form an inverted T with both knees bent; the toes of the left foot point toward the outside of the right foot. As your right foot steps outward, the left heel raises to allow the sharp angled turn. The toes of the right foot are on the line of the circle. Then the left foot steps forward on the same line as your right and comes to rest beside it. The distance between your two feet should be sufficiently wide for a stable stance (figure 27).

*Figure 27*

2. Shift your weight onto your left hip. The left palm is held just behind the left ear with the palm facing downward and the fingers pointing toward the ear. Then twist your waist to the right and lift the right leg, keeping the thigh level and the toes pointing toward the floor. At the same time your right palm, still facing downward, shoots under the left armpit as the left palm slices outward to the front. The palm shape, bend of the arm, and feeling of being inwardly wrapped and outwardly stretched are just like those of the entering movement of the Crouching Tiger form. In this left one-legged stance, keep your knee slightly bent for a more stable base (figure 28).

*Figure 28*

3. To return to the circle, the left palm pushes to the outside, both twisting and lifting. The right palm twists into a Right Ward-Off movement. Kick out with the right foot on the line of the circle synchronized with the Ward-Off maneuver. The rest of the form is just like the ending of the Single Palm Change.

4. To perform Yellow Dragon Rolls Over on the other side, simply reverse the right and left movements in the directions above.

## The Complete Sequence of Yellow Dragon Rolls Over

Figure 4-1

Figure 4-2

Figure 4-3

Figure 4-4

Figure 4-4 (front view)

Figure 4-5

*Figure 4-6*

*Figure 4-7*

*Dragon counters Tiger*

▬▬  ▬▬
▬▬  ▬▬   Yellow Dragon Rolls Over: In almost all Bagua Zhang styles the kun
▬▬▬▬▬▬   trigram personifies a twisting, spiraling form that often differs consider-
ably from the other changes. Kun is usually associated with a mythical beast such as
a Chinese dragon or Chinese unicorn (part lion and part deer). Yellow Dragon Rolls
Over is the only one of the eight changes that opens by spinning away from the center
of the circle. Kun, with its three broken lines, is pure yin in nature. Yielding is the
key to its execution, and no one part of the body is accentuated over another. Yellow
Dragon personifies attack hidden within defense. The palm shape is qie, or slicing,
and the action is pi, or splitting. You break the opponent's structure by attacking both
high (slicing palm) and low (heel kick) at the same time. Practice it so the upper and
lower body are completely coordinated both inwardly and outwardly.

Yi Jing Connection: Kun is of the earth. It is soft and obedient, the opposite of
qian. Kun is pure yin in character and is smooth and fluid. It is likened to the purity
of a mare. Kun often complements the creative rather than opposing it. In human
relations qian is related to the firmness of the father, and kun to the softness of the
mother. There is no advance, no retreat. Kun can counteract qian.

# Fifth Palm Form: "White Snake Spits Out Tongue"

1. As you walk the circle on the right side, step forward firmly with the right foot transferring all the weight to the right hip. The left foot [inside foot] takes a half step forward, touching the toes down lightly. The left forearm twists upward until level with the forehead with a feeling of being inwardly wrapped and outwardly stretched. The right palm does not move (figure 29).

*Figure 29*

2. With the right hand and foot as your center point, use your waist power to turn backward and to the left. While you are twisting the waist, turn the left palm outward and upward, circling it back and over your head, and twist the arm too (figure 30). The palm faces upward and fingers forward; keep the palm heel under the chin and drop the elbow to protect the chest. The right palm turns upward with the inner palm touching the hip. Weight the right foot and turn the knee inward—like the rear leg of Crouching Tiger. Touch the ball of the left foot down in front and to the left of the right foot. The left heel and right instep are separated by the width of a fist (figure 31).

*Figure 30*                    *Figure 31*

3. Take a half step forward with the left foot; at the same time shoot out the left palm. Stay weighted on the rear foot (figure 32).

4. Turn the toes of the left foot out as you parry down and outward with the left palm. The right palm, facing upward, shoots out from under the chin and over the left hand—just like the changing palm of Crouching Tiger. You remain rear-weighted.

*Figure 32*

5. Hook the toes of the right foot inward [kou] until you form a number-8 stance (/\). Turn the waist and neck toward the left. Both palms remain in the same position and turn inward.

6. Continuing from above, as the waist turns left, the left foot lifts slightly off the ground and takes a step backward, brushing the right ankle as it goes.

Use the heel of the right foot as your pivot point on the left turn. When you finish, the feet should be in the position shown (figure 33). As you turn, the left palm moves along the front chest, both leading and twisting, until it reaches the far left side. Then twist and turn your left palm upward to a point just above your head to protect the forehead. Keep the arm bent and the elbow facing left. At the same time, the right palm follows the left waist turn and pierces forward, with the fingers twisting upward and outward and the wrist pressing forward (figure 34).

Figure 33                     Figure 34

7. Turn back on the circle as in the Single Palm Change. To perform White Snake Spits Out Tongue on the left side, simply reverse right and left movements.

*Figure 5-1*

*Figure 5-2*

*Figure 5-3*

*Figure 5-4*

*Figure 5-5*

*Figure 5-6*

*Figure 5-7*

*Figure 5-8*

*Figure 5-9*

*Figure 5-10*

*Figure 5-11*

*Figure 5-12*

*Figure 5-13*

*Figure 5-14*

*Figure 5-15*

*Figure 5-16*

White Snake Spits Out Tongue, the fifth palm change in Wang Shujin's Bagua Linking Palms form, is represented by the kan trigram. Like the trigram itself the change is firm (yang) in the center and flexible (yin) on the outside. Its movements have the appearance of softness while keeping a strong inner core. The practitioner feels outwardly stretched and internally wrapped throughout the form. Kan's nature is that of flowing water, which is soft to the touch but has a firmness due to its mass and speed.

White Snake's palm is called tuo, or carrying, because it enters softly, lifts the opponent to the point of imbalance, then strikes swiftly like a snake. The palm change ends by coiling about the opponent and throwing him off to the side. If the movements of White Snake are done correctly, Wang Shujin remarked that the Qi will become full and you will "elevate the heart's fire." If performed incorrectly, water in the kidneys will void, you will become dizzy, and your vision will blur.

Yi Jing Connection: Kan is related to danger. Water flows from above but does not fill—as in a waterfall crashing into a rushing stream. Danger is at hand, but you remain safe by holding your heart's strength inside and proceeding through trouble unharmed. The time is dangerous; be cautious and await the appointed hour. A step forward or backward leads to more danger; follow the line of least resistance. The opposite of kan is li.

# Sixth Palm Form: "Mighty Peng Spreads Wings"

1. As you walk the circle on the right, make a hooking step, or kou bu, with the right foot, twisting the waist to the right, and transferring weight to the right hip while bending both knees. The left palm does not change but follows the waist turn until the palm is in front of the right side of the face. The right palm does not move (figure 35).

*Figure 35*          *Figure 36*

2. Twist your waist left and step forward with the left foot. The left palm, edge leading, sweeps low like a pendulum, passing the left knee, and ending at face height on the left side. The palm faces away, and the fingers point forward. The right hand turns palm up and rests below the right ribs (figure 36).

3. Step forward with the right foot forming a hooking step in front of the left. The right hand forms a Cow's Tongue hand and hides behind the right buttock (figure 37). Twist the waist to the left. The left palm turns over following the leftward turn, passes over the head, and cuts downward to the left side. The left leg is carried along by the turn and takes a big step out to the left; the toes touch down firmly and smoothly.

*Figure 37*

The right hand forms an open palm, sweeps upward toward the left front like a wheel, and chops past the left palm. During this movement the shoulders stay relaxed, the arms soft, and the elbows bent. The chop is brisk and powerful, and the palms, waist, and feet move in unison. The left palm slaps past the right and stops by the right cheek with the elbows protecting the chest. The back of the left palm is held near the face with the fingers pointing upward. Squat down with both legs but remain slightly rear-weighted. As the palms cross in the chopping movement, the rear knee hooks inward (figure 38).

4. Next, the left palm pushes outward and supports as the right palm pene-trates and twists. Lift the right leg and extend it outward just like the Single Palm Change; however, the arms do not form Right Ward-Off but rather cross like Cross Hands in Taiji Quan. When the arms separate, the right first rises and falls while the left descends. The elbows and wrists remain bent, wrapped, and outwardly stretched. The two arms form a semicircle with both palms vertical, like Great Peng spreading its wings and soaring (figure 39).

Figure 38                    Figure 39

5. To perform Mighty Peng Spreads Wings on the left side, just exchange right and left movements.

*Figure 6-1*

*Figure 6-2*

*Figure 6-3*

*Figure 6-4*

*Figure 6-5*

Figure 6-6                    Figure 6-6 (front view)

Figure 6-7            Figure 6-8            Figure 6-8 (alternate move)

*Figure 6-9*               *Figure 6-10*               *Figure 6-11*

*Figure 6-12*               *Figure 6-13*

Mighty Peng Spreads Wings: Peng is a giant bird of Chinese Daoist legend, similar to the roc of western mythology. Chuang Tzu said that Mighty Peng could rise on the wind and soar for a thousand *li* without flapping its wings. Peng truly knew the art of effortless doing. The spreading of Peng's wings is represented in the gen trigram's two broken yin lines below. The solid yang line above represents the powerful overhand blow that cocks above the head and crashes downward in a chopping motion.

Several palm shapes are used in the change, including grasping palm, thrusting palm, and the ox tongue palm—not really a palm but more like the "beak hand" in Taiji Quan's Single Whip. The main action involved in Mighty Peng Spreads Wings is the difficult to translate *dai*. Dai means to connect with something and carry it along. The larger movements of Mighty Peng Spreads Wings are manifested in the opening and closing of the arms and spreading of the back that evokes wing-like images.

The gen trigram carries with it the symbol of a mountain. Peng represents the largeness of a mountain along with the character of "keeping still" as it rides on the wind. Again we find the concept of stillness in movement. Both Wang Shujin and Sun Lutang said that if this change is done correctly, your "heart Qi will descend to the dantian."

Yi Jing Connection: Gen's image is that of a mountain. Its character is that of brightness and light. With yang on the top and yin below, the potential for movement is downward. Gen's energy indicates stopping in time and proceeding at the right time. Move at the right moment, and the way will be bright. The opposite of gen is dui.

# Seventh Palm Form: "White Ape Presents Peaches"

1. As you walk the circle on the right, toe-in with the right foot, forming a hooking step, or kou bu, with the left toes pointing to the right instep. Twist the waist leftward and solidly weight the right hip. Both palms follow the left waist turn. The arms twist outward, separating and describing a circle, and return to rest with the inner edges of the upturned palms on each side of the abdomen. Keep the shoulders relaxed and the elbows bent throughout; the chest and back remain rounded. Pull back the left leg, touching down the toes, and lower the body while balancing on the right leg (figure 40).

*Figure 40*

2. From there, the two palms meet together and slowly lift upward. When the palms near the chin, send them straight outward to the front (White Ape Presents Peaches). The palms should be level with the eyes, and the elbows drop to protect the chest. As the palms project forward, the body slowly rises, lifting the left leg up until the thigh is level with the floor; the lower leg hangs and the toes point downward. The left foot protects the right knee (figure 41).

3. Continuing on from there, both palms turn inward and away until the Tiger's Mouths [thumb to index finger] are facing each other and protecting the sides of the forehead. This is like the Lion Holds Ball posture [see figure 7-10]. Next, the left foot steps down just to the outside of the circle, the right foot follows, and you continue walking as before (figure 42).

*Figure 41*                                    *Figure 42*

4. To perform White Ape Presents Peaches on the left side, exchange right and left movements.

Figure 7-1

Figure 7-2

Figure 7-3

Figure 7-4

Figure 7-5

Figure 7-6

Figure 7-7

Figure 7-8

Figure 7-9

Figure 7-10

*Figure 7-1 (alternate)*

*Figure 7-2 (alternate)*

*Figure 7-3 (alternate)*

*Figure 7-4 (alternate)*

*Figure 7-5 (alternate)*

*Figure 7-6 (alternate)*

*Figure 7-7 (alternate)*          *Figure 7-8 (alternate)*          *Figure 7-9 (alternate)*

White Ape Presents Peaches: The dui trigram is represented by the symbol of a swamp or lake. Water (yin) collects above and is supported by the lake bottom and bedrock (yang) below. The palm change also shows soft, flowing handwork above with the waist and legs providing solid support. The action is one of jin, or entering. You crouch like a monkey, use guile to avoid a direct attack, then spring up suddenly and penetrate forward, attacking both high and low. According to Wang Shujin, if White Ape is performed correctly, the lung's Qi will be clear and rich. If done incorrectly, you will pant and cough.

Yi Jing Connection: Dui is represented by a swamp. Strength and resolve within are expressed outwardly by yielding and softness. Dui is open in character but keeps a firm center to prevent danger from penetrating. Opposite of dui is gen.

# Eighth Palm Form: "Whirlwind Palms"

1. As you walk the circle on the right side in the Lion Holds Ball posture, toe-in with the right foot. Squat down slightly on both legs, and press down-ward with both palms, with the fingers of the left hand pointing toward the center of the circle (figure 43).

2. Twist the waist to the left as both palms turn to face upward, with the fingers of the left hand pointing directly toward the center of the circle (figure 44). The arms remain rounded, the elbows hanging, and the forearms level. At the same time, the left foot steps straight forward while the body remains weighted mostly on the back leg.

Figure 43

Figure 44

3. From there, step slightly forward with the left foot while turning the toes outward. The left hand turns over with the palm facing downward. The wrist is wrapped and the arm is rounded like the forward palm in Crouching Tiger. The palms have the feeling of covering (figure 45). Next, the right foot steps straight past the open left foot, and at the same time the right palm passes in front of the mouth, and over the back of the left palm, penetrating forward like the rear palm of Crouching Tiger in Double Palm Change. The left foot shuffles in and touches the toes down, adhering to the back of the right leg. Both knees are bent (figure 46).

4. Continue by twisting the waist to the left rear, and follow by lifting the left leg and taking a long step back to the left rear, stepping down firmly. At the same time the left palm brushes past the left knee and rises as if following the circumference of a wheel back toward the right side. Just as the

*Figure 45*

*Figure 46*

left leg sets down, bend the left arm and press out with the elbow, keeping the palm downward. The right palm follows and ends under the left palm, facing upward. Shift weight to the front leg [bow stance] and the palms protect the abdomen with the intention of embracing (figure 47).

5. Next, twist the waist right while shifting weight to the right foot. Both arms swing low to the right following the waist. Twist the waist back to the left as the arms rise in a wheel-like motion to the left side. As the arms descend left, shift the weight back to the right, turning the waist right; then slide the left foot over to adhere to the right leg with the toes down. At the same time, the right palm chops out right with the arm level and bent inward. The left arm follows to the right side in a supporting movement with the palm facing right and the fingers pointing down and away (figure 48).

*Figure 47*                    *Figure 48*

6. Then twist the waist left and toe-out left, taking a half-step outward (figure 49). The right foot follows and hooks inward. The waist continues turning left, and the left foot opens into a leftward step. Both palms turn over with the left chopping out to the left and the right supporting, as in the previous posture. The stance is like Crouching Tiger with more weight on the rear leg (figure 50).

7. Next, the left palm pushes, twists, and presses outward as the right palm penetrates under the left shoulder. Shuffle the right foot in and perform Right Ward-Off just like the Single Palm Change.

8. To end the form here, as you finish Right Ward-Off, step down with both feet side by side as in the opening movements of the form. Both palms return to the chest and press downward until they reach your hips, as in the beginning posture. To do the form on the left side, walk the circle in the Lion Holds Ball posture and exchange right and left movements as above.

Figure 49                                    Figure 50

*Figure 8-1*

*Figure 8-2*

*Figure 8-3*

*Figure 8-4*

*Figure 8-5*

*Figure 8-6*

*Figure 8-7*

*Figure 8-8*

*Figure 8-9*

*Figure 8-10*

*Figure 8-11*

*Figure 8-12*

*Figure 8-13*          *Figure 8-14*          *Figure 8-15*

*Figure 8-16*

*Figure 8-17*

*Figure 8-18*

*Figure 8-19*

*Figure 8-20*

*Figure 8-21*

Whirlwind Palms is one of the most difficult Bagua Zhang attacks to defend against. The strength of the movements is mirrored in the xun trigram. Two yang lines above represent the strong unceasing rotation of the arms and waist; the yin line below evokes the agility of the legwork. The overall action is ban, which means to pick something up and move it about. This eighth change of Bagua Linked Palms is the only one that moves across the center while performing two 360-degree spins. This is one reason the change is also referred to as "Eight Immortals Crossing the Sea."

The arm movements of Whirlwind Palms are like that of a windmill. When the spinning upper body movements are combined with circular leg work, one can easily see how the name of this palm form arose. Wang Shujin's disciple, Huang Jinsheng, likened the Bagua Zhang practitioner to the eye of a hurricane. The mind remains unmoved in the calm eye of the storm, while the swirling maelstrom of arms and legs rages without. Wang said if Whirlwind Palms is performed smoothly, Qi will penetrate to the extremities. Your movements will be as flowing and unbroken as the wind.

Yi Jing Connection: Xun is represented by wind. Yin on bottom is docile and obedient. It is trapped underneath double yang and cannot escape. Like branches blown by the wind it must bend and obey or be broken. Xun penetrates like wind blowing through trees and roots growing through earth—not forceful but incessant. The opposite of xun is zhen.

# Glossary

Ba Bu (八步): Eight Stance, a Bagua stance that turns the toes inward resembling the two brush strokes that form the Chinese character ba (八)

Bafan Quan (八番拳): Eight Turns/Changes Boxing

bagua (八卦): Eight trigrams, the basic building blocks of the sixty-four hexagrams of the Yi Jing

Bagua Zhang (八卦掌): Eight Trigrams Palm (or Eight Trigrams Boxing)

Bai Bu (擺步): Opening or Swinging Step, a step that opens outward away from the body

ban (搬): To move about (in a large area)

Cang Jie (倉頡): Circa 2650 BCE; legendary inventor of Chinese characters

Cheng Ming Martial Arts School (誠明國術管): A school founded by Wang Shujin

Cheng Tinghua (程廷華): 1848–1900; a student of Dong Haiquan

Chen Panling (陳泮嶺): 1892–1967; a mentor and collaborator of Wang Shujin

chuanchu (轉註): Using the definition of things

Cun Bu (寸步): Inch Step

dai (帶): To carry

Da Mo Zhuang (達摩樁): Bodhidharma Stance

dantian (丹田): The "field of elixir" located just below the navel

Dian Bu (墊步): Sinking Step

Ding Bu (丁步): T Step, a Bagua step in which the toes of the back foot point toward the instep of the front, resembling the Chinese character ding (丁)

Dong Haiquan (董海川): 1796–1880; developer of the martial art Bagua Zhang

Fu Xi (伏犧): Mythical Chinese emperor credited with writing the Book of Changes

Gua Bu (過步): Continuous Step

Gu Jici (古磯子): A legendary Daoist adept said to have taught Dong Haiquan

gun (棍): A wooden staff or cudgel

He Luo Classic (河洛圖書): Luo (River) Classic, an ancient book of mathematical divination (also known as Luo Shu)

Hsing Men (行門): Hsing Men Boxing

Huan Xi Zhuang (歡喜椿): Joyful Stance

Hu Zuo Zhuang (虎座椿): Crouching Tiger Stance

Hong Quan (洪拳): Hong (family) Boxing

Hong Yimian (洪懿棉): One of two Taiwanese brothers who studied with Zhang Junfong

Hong Yixiang (洪懿祥): One of two Taiwanese brothers who studied with Zhang Junfong

Hou Zhenyuan (侯震遠): Said to be the martial arts instructor of a Manchu prince

Huang Jinsheng (黃金生): Disciple of Wang Shujin; Yi Guan Daoist leader in Taiwan

huiyi (會意): Using the meanings of things

jiajie (假借): Borrowing categories

Jian Bu (剪步): Scissor Step

jin (進): To enter

Jingong Quan (金工拳): Metalwork Boxing

kou (扣): To hook or to button

Kou Bu (扣步): Hooking Step or Button Step, a step that turns toes and knees inward

kua (跨): The area of the pelvic girdle, hips

li (力): Physical or muscular strength

Liang Zhenpu (梁振普): 1863–1932; a student of Dong Haiquan

liang'yi (兩儀): Positive and negative symbols, written as —— and — —

Liao Zhang (撩掌): Scooping Palm

Li Cunyi (李存義): 1849–1921; a student of Dong Haiquan

ling (領): To lead

Liu Dekuan (劉的寬): died 1911; a student of Dong Haiquan

Liu Fengchun (劉鳳春): 1855–1922; a student of Dong Haiquan

Li Zhang (立掌): Vertical Palm

lulu guan (轆轤關): An acupuncture point located between the shoulder blades

Lung Men (龍門): Dragon Gate, a sect of Daoism

Luo Shu (洛書): Luo (River) Classic, an ancient book of mathematical divination (also known as the He Luo Classic)

Ma Guei (馬貴): 1854–1940; a student of Dong Haiquan

Ma Weiqi (馬維旗): 1851–1880; a student of Dong Haiquan

Meng Zi (孟子): 372–289 BCE; a Chinese philosopher and interpreter of Confucianism

Mt. Ermei (峨嵋山): A mountain in Sichuan Province

Mt. Luo Jia (洛加山): A mountain near Mt. Ermei

Niushi Zhang (牛舌掌): Cow's Tongue Palm

niwan (泥丸): An acupuncture point located between the eyebrows peng (掤): A special martial arts term usually translated as "ward off"

pi (劈): To split

Pi Zhang (劈掌): Splitting Palm

Qi (氣): Vapor, breath, air; in martial and healing arts, used to mean energy or life essence

Qie Zhang (切掌): Slicing Palm

Quan Zhen Dao (全真道): Complete Truth/Reality Way; a Daoist sect

Shang Daoyuan (尚道元): A legendary Daoist adept said to have taught Dong Haiquan

Shi Baoshan (史寶山): Dates unknown; a student of Dong Haiquan

Shuang Fen Zhuang (雙分椿): Double Separation Post Stance

Shuang Peng Zhuang (雙掤椿): Double Ward-Off Post Stance

Shuang Tui Zhuang (雙推椿): Double Push Post Stance

Shun Bu Dan Peng Zhuang (順步單掤椿): Smooth Step Single Ward-Off Post Stance

Shun Bu Shuang Peng Zhuang (順步雙掤椿): Smooth Step Double Ward-Off Post Stance

Silian Quan (四連拳): Four Continuous Boxing

si'xiang (思象): Four shapes making up all possible combinations of —— and —— stacked on top of each other (e.g., ==)

Sung Changrong (宋長榮): Dates unknown; a student of Dong Haiquan

Sung Yongxiang (宋永祥): Dates unknown; a student of Dong Haiquan

Sun Xikun (孫錫堃): 1883–1952; a student of Cheng Youlong, the son of Cheng Tinghua

taiji (太極): Light and shadow as symbolized by the yin-yang diagram

Taiji Quan (太極拳): Great Ultimate Boxing

Three Bao (三抱): Embrace, hold

Three Chui (三垂): Hang down, drop

Three Ding (三頂): Highest, outermost point

Three Kou (三扣): Clamp, compress

Three Min (三敏): Alert, sensitive, quick

Three Qu (三曲): Bend, curve

Three Ting (三挺): Straighten, pull up

Three Yuan (三圓): Round, wrap

Tiao Zhang (挑掌): Lifting Palm

tui (推): To push

tuo (托): To lift

Tuo Zhang (托掌): Carrying Palm

Wang Xiangzhai (王薌齋): 1885–1963; credited with founding Yi Quan and Dacheng Quan; one of Wang Shujin's teachers

weilu guan (尾關): An acupuncture point located near the base of the skull

wuji (無極): Formlessness, void; the state of the universe before separating into the positive and negative forces of yin and yang; a standing posture in Bagua Zhang

Wu Mengxia (吳孟挾): A Bagua Zhang instructor and Yi Guan Daoist

xiangxin (象形): Using the shapes of things

Xian Tian Da Dao (先天大道): Great Way of Pre-Heaven; a precursor to Yi Guan Dao in Mainland China

Xiao Haibo (蕭海波): 1863–1954; one of Wang Shujin's teachers

xingshen (形聲): Imitating the sound of things

Xingyi Quan (形意拳): Form-Mind Boxing

yi (義): Will, intent

Yi Guan Dao (一貫道): Way of One Unity; a syncretic religious sect that adheres to mostly Daoist, Buddhist, and Confucian tenets

Yin Fu (尹福): 1842–1911; a student of Dong Haiquan

Yi Quan (義拳): A quasi-martial discipline based on standing meditation, founded by Wang Xiangzhai

yuzhen guan (玉枕關): An acupuncture point located on the back of the head

Zhang Junfong (張俊峰): 1902–1974; martial artist and friend of Wang Shujin

Zhang Sanfeng (張三丰): The legendary Daoist often credited with developing Taiji Quan

Zhang Zhaodong (張兆東): 1859–1940; a student of Dong Haiquan; one of Wang Shujin's teachers

Zhan Zhuang (站樁): Standing on posts, a style of standing meditation

Zhou Yisen (週義森): Yi Guan Daoist leader who sponsored Wang Shujin in Taiwan

Zhuan Zhang (轉掌): Rotating Palms, an early name for Bagua Zhang

zishi (指示): Pointing to symbols

zuan (穿): To drill or penetrate by moving the fingers forward while rotating the hand from a palm down to palm up position

Zuan Zhang (穿掌): Piercing Palm

# References

---
*Commentary: A Closer Look at Wang Shujin*
---

"An Introduction to Wang Shu Jin and His Ba Gua Zhang." *Pa Kua Chang Journal* 5, no. 6 (September/October 1995):3–7.

---
*Commentary: A Modern Look at Master Dong Haiquan*
---

Kang Gewu. *The Complete Practical Book of Chinese Martial Arts, Taiwan Edition.* 2000, 88–122. (In Chinese)

"The Life of Tung Hai-Ch'uan and the History of His Tomb." *Pa Kua Chang Journal* 3, no. 1 (November/December 1992):3–13.

"The Origins of Pa Kua Chang: Part One." *Pa Kua Chang Journal* 3, no. 1 (November/December 1992):14–20.

"The Origins of Pa Kua Chang: Part Two." *Pa Kua Chang Journal* 3, no. 2 (January/February 1993):14–22.

"The Origins of Pa Kua Chang: Part Three." *Pa Kua Chang Journal* 3, no. 4 (May/June 1993):25–30.

---
*Yi Jing Commentaries in Bagua Linked Palms*
---

Blofeld, J. *The Book of Changes: A New Translation of the Ancient Chinese I Ching.* New York: E.P. Dutton, 1965.

Chou Jen-tse, ed. *Jou Yi* [Book of Changes]. Taipei: Caves Books, 1981. (In Chinese)

Huang Ch'ing-I. *Jou Yi Du Ben* [Book of Changes Reader]. Taipei: Taiwan University San Min Publishing, 1980. (In Chinese)

# About the Authors

KENT HOWARD is a nationally known writer and martial arts teacher who resides in Chico, California. He has a degree in East Asian Languages and spent over twenty years directing English as a Second Language programs in Asia and the United States. Kent has been practicing Chinese martial arts for more than thirty years and is considered an authority on Bagua Zhang and Taoism. He studied internal martial arts under Taoist master Huang Jinsheng, a close disciple of Wang Shujin. Kent is the author of numerous articles on Chinese martial arts and philosophy, and was a former contributor to the esteemed *Pa Kua Chang Journal*. He is presently working on an introduction to the modern system of Nonviolent Self Defense (NSD) as well as the translation of Wang Shujin's second book.

CHEN HSIAO-YEN is an artist, translator, and writer from Taiwan. She graduated from Soo Chow University with a degree in Chinese Literature and did post-graduate work in fine arts in the U.S. She has had a long association with Taoism and Bagua Zhang. Her latest project is a children's book called *Red Dragon Bridge*, which she is writing and illustrating. She lives with Kent Howard, her husband, in Chico, California.

---

*For additional materials and instructional DVDs on Wang Shujin's Bagua Zhang, as well as information on upcoming Bagua Zhang seminars, please visit www.bagualinkedpalms.com.*

---